EYE SEE

It's a dog's life!

I'm Sparky the dog and I'd like to welcome you to *Eye See!* I hope you're all bright-eyed and bushy-tailed like me, because this edition of *The Navigator* is all about the things you see in the world around you. On your travels through its pages, you'll come across some puzzling pictures that prove that things are not always as they first seem. You'll also get the chance to meet some of my furry animal friends, including my canine chum, Skylar the search and rescue dog. You can also go underwater in search of a lost city.

Don't worry, you're in safe hands – dogs are great swimmers!

Text Type	Literacy Skills	Wider Curriculum Links
Explanation/ Persuasive	Close reading of visual information; reading sequentially; linking text and visuals	**Geography** Unit 8: Improving the environment
Recount	Close reading for detail; summarising information; linking and synthesising information	**History** Unit 10: What can we find out about ancient Egypt?
Report	Close reading of visual information; making comparisons; linking text and visuals	**Geography** Unit 9: Village settlers
Explanation	Linking text and visuals; finding information in text and visuals; close reading for detail	**Science** Unit 4A: Moving and growing
Report	Close reading of visual information; skimming; scanning; making comparisons; linking text and visuals	**History** Unit 9: What was it like for children in the Second World War?
Report	Linking and synthesising information; interpreting visuals; deductive comprehension	**Science** Unit 4B: Habitats
Persuasive/ Explanation	Close reading of visual information; making comparisons; deductive comprehension; interpreting data	**Design and Technology** Unit 4A: Money containers
Persuasive/ Explanation	Close reading of visual information; linking text and visuals; expressing and justifying an opinion	**Design and Technology** Unit 4A: Money containers
Report	Close reading of visual information; making comparisons; reflecting; expressing and justifying an opinion	
Recount	Close reading; linking information; reflecting	
Fun spread		
		ICT: Year 4 Schemes of work

ALUMINIUM - NEW

How many cans of drink do you have in a week? What do you do when the can is empty? Do you throw it away? But stop! Most cans are made from aluminium, and can easily be recycled. This is how:

1. The new cans are filled. Their contents are drunk.

1

2

2. Empty aluminium cans are collected in can banks.

6

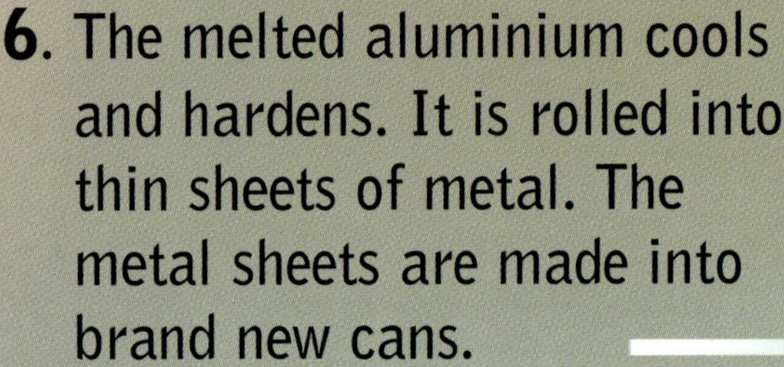

6. The melted aluminium cools and hardens. It is rolled into thin sheets of metal. The metal sheets are made into brand new cans.

ALUMINIUM FACT FILE

What is aluminium?

Aluminium is a metal which is used to make drinks cans, cooking foil and many other things.

How is it made?

Aluminium is made from a rock called bauxite. The bauxite is dug up in quarries. It is then crushed and heated in a factory to produce aluminium.

CANS FROM OLD

3. The cans are collected from the banks. They are sorted and crushed into bales.

4. The bales are taken to a recycling factory.

5. The bales are heated until they melt. The melted aluminium is poured into a giant mould.

It takes 20 times more electricity to make new cans from bauxite than from recycled cans.

So what's the problem?

Making aluminium damages the environment, uses a lot of energy and pollutes the air. It is also very expensive.

What can we do?

Don't throw your empty aluminium cans away. Recycle them instead.

THE MYSTERY OF THE DISAPPEARING CITY

A MYSTERIOUS EVENT

2000 years ago, an Egyptian city called Herakleion stood at the mouth of the River Nile. Ancient Egyptian writings tell us that Herakleion was a rich, busy city full of beautiful palaces, gardens and temples. Then suddenly, about 1300 years ago, Herakleion disappeared. What could have happened? This mystery has baffled historians for hundreds of years.

FINDING HERAKLEION

In 1996, a French archaeologist called Franck Goddio decided to find the lost city of Herakleion. First, he and his team learned as much as they could about the city. They looked at old maps of the area. After examining all the evidence, they decided on a likely spot to start looking for the city.

HIDDEN TREASURE

The archaeologists used a machine called a magnetometer to help them to find the city. This machine told them that there were lots of metal objects buried under the seabed. Could these objects belong to the lost city of Herakleion?

A CITY FROZEN IN TIME

Next, divers swam down to the seabed to find out more. Slowly and carefully, the divers sifted through the sand. Eventually, they made an amazing discovery. Under the seabed was the entire city of Herakleion, with its buildings and city walls still standing. Franck Goddio announced that they had found, "an intact city, frozen in time".

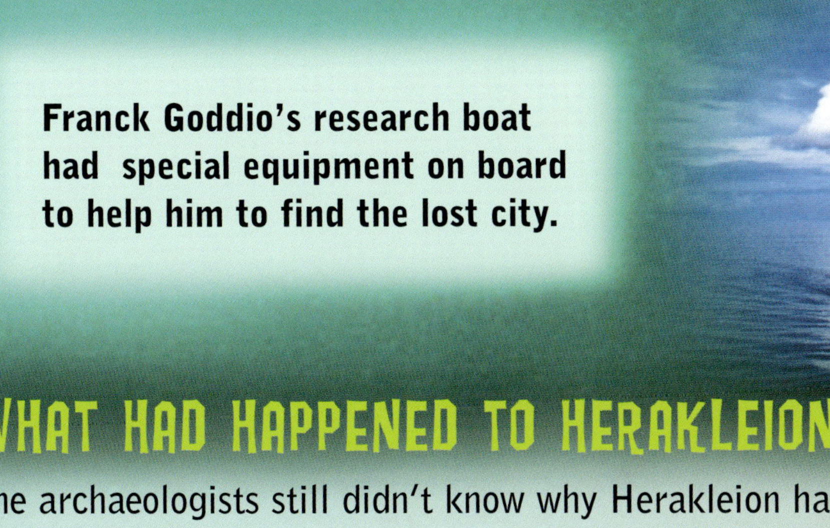

Franck Goddio's research boat had special equipment on board to help him to find the lost city.

WHAT HAD HAPPENED TO HERAKLEION?

The archaeologists still didn't know why Herakleion had disappeared. They asked the divers to continue their search of the city. The divers used underwater cameras to take photographs and videos. They also brought some objects to the surface to show the archaeologists.

The archaeologists pieced together all these clues. They worked out that Herakleion had been hit by a huge earthquake. They knew this because the walls of the city were all leaning in the same direction, which suggests that the city was struck by a huge force. Thanks to the hard work of the archaeologists and divers, the mystery of the disappearing city was finally solved!

The dates on these gold coins helped the archaeologists to find out when Herakleion had disappeared.

Rutland under water

Church at Nether Hambleton

Flooded

Rutland is the smallest county in England, but nearly 30 years ago it was chosen as the site for one of the largest reservoirs in Europe. The reservoir (called Rutland Water) was needed to supply fresh water to growing towns such as Northampton and Peterborough. However, building the reservoir involved the loss of farmland, moving people from their homes and flooding the tiny village of Nether Hambleton.

ORDNANCE SURVEY MAP, 1974

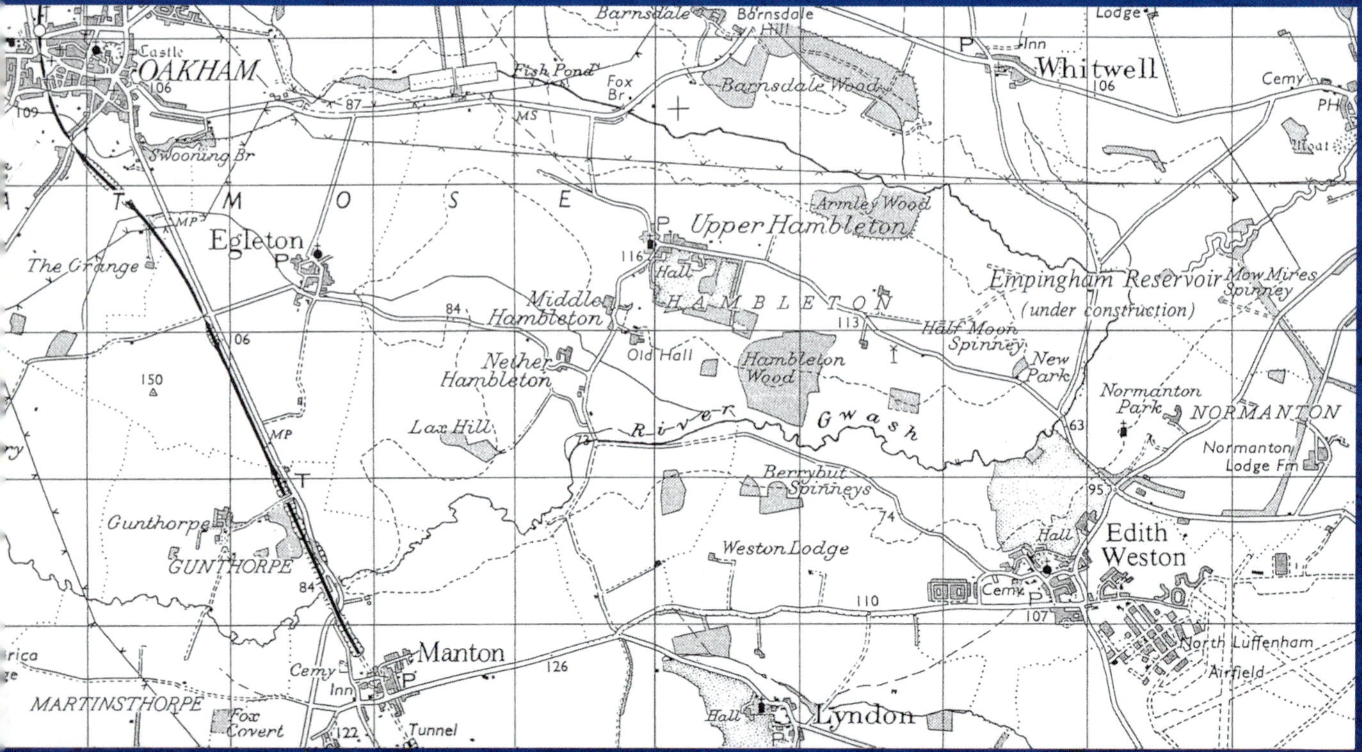

Protests

At first local people, newspapers and landowners fought to stop the reservoir being built. At the time people signed petitions, held protest marches and stood in the way of bulldozers to delay building work.

Rutland & Sta

BATTLE IS JOINED OVER RUTLAND RESERVOIR

County authorities combine t fight the Empingham schem

Essendine school to close soon

Tickencote fatal mars holiday we end on local ro

Different views

In the years since the reservoir was created, many people's views of Rutland Water have changed dramatically. People now travel from miles around to fish or sail on the water, or to eat a picnic on the shore. Local people are now proud of Rutland Water and the many new attractions it brought to the area.

For instance, not far from the site of flooded Nether Hambleton is the internationally famous Rutland Water Nature Reserve. The Nature Reserve is deeply involved in breeding rare birds, and is one of the only places in England where the beautiful osprey can be seen.

ORDNANCE SURVEY MAP, 1999

'DON'T FLOOD RUTLAND'
Slogan is adopted for fight against giant reservoir

"DON'T FLOOD Rutland" is to be the slogan of the Rutland branch of the Council for the Preservation of Rural England in their fight against the proposed 27,000 million gallon reservoir between ...ham and Empingham covering 3,114 acres.

Rutland Water

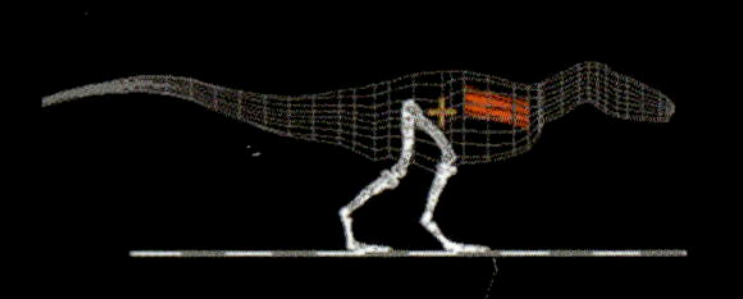

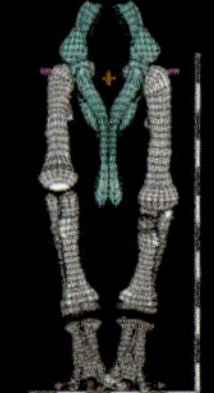

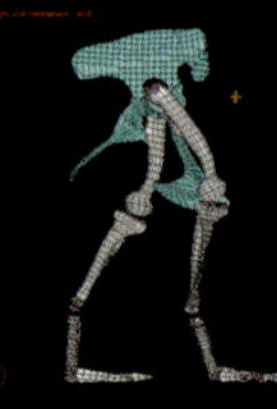

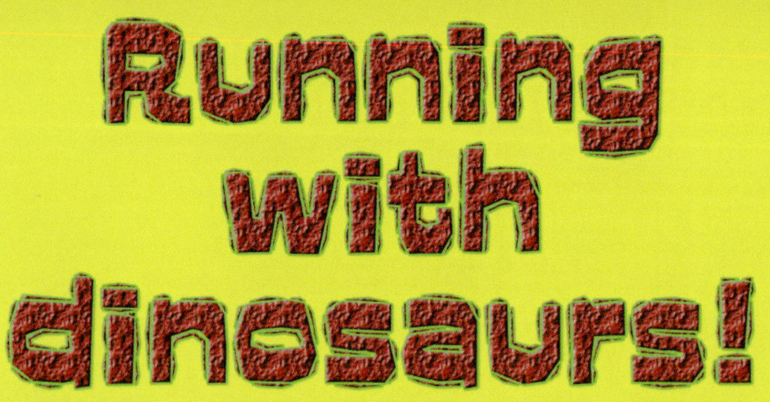

Running with dinosaurs!

Dinosaur experts are known as palaeontologists. By studying dinosaur footprints and comparing them to tracks left by modern animals, they make predictions about how dinosaurs moved.

THE BARE BONES

If palaeontologists work out what a dinosaur's skeleton and muscles looked like, this can give them clues about how a dinosaur might have moved. If they know the size and position of the vertebrae in the spine, they can predict how the dinosaur moved its body and head. In the same way, the length, shape and number of leg bones can help them work out how the dinosaur walked.

THE STEGOSAURUS MAY HAVE REARED UPON ITS HIND LEGS TO REACH VEGETATION.

long stiff tail

short front legs

straight, long back legs which sprawled out to the sides

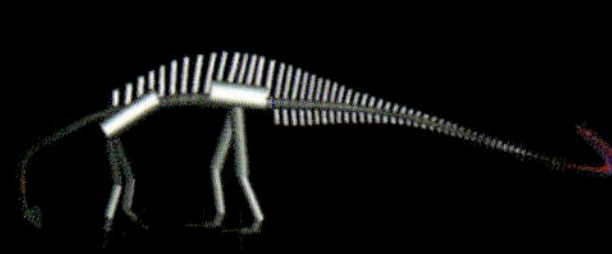

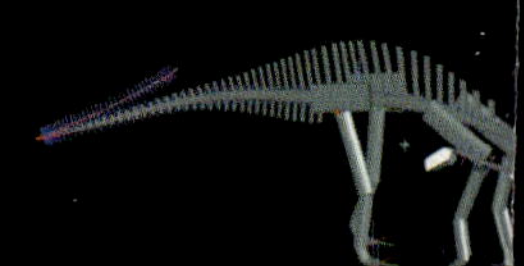

TWO LEGS OR FOUR?

Dinosaurs can be classified into two groups: quadrupeds (dinosaurs that walked on four legs) and bipeds (dinosaurs that walked on two legs). However, some quadrupeds used two legs when running so they could move faster.

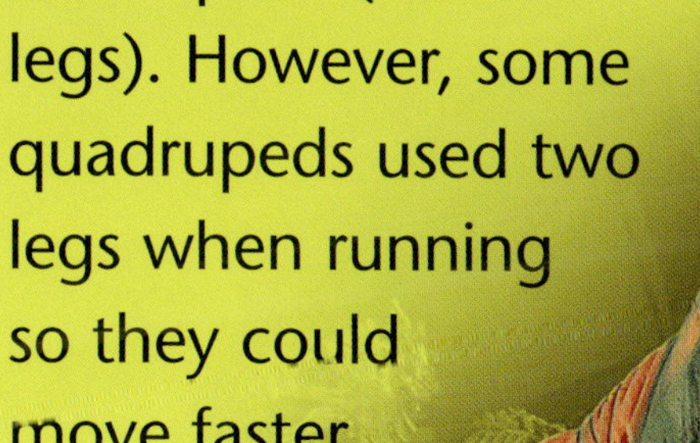

strong, powerful back legs

Bipedal dinosaurs	Quadrupedal dinosaurs
Acrocanthosaurus	Ankylosaurus
Ceratosaurus	Brachiosaurus
Compsognathus	Diplodocus
Giganotosaurus	Plateosaurus
Megaraptor	Seismosaurus
Oviraptor	Stegosaurus
Tyrannosaurus rex	Triceratops
Velociraptor	

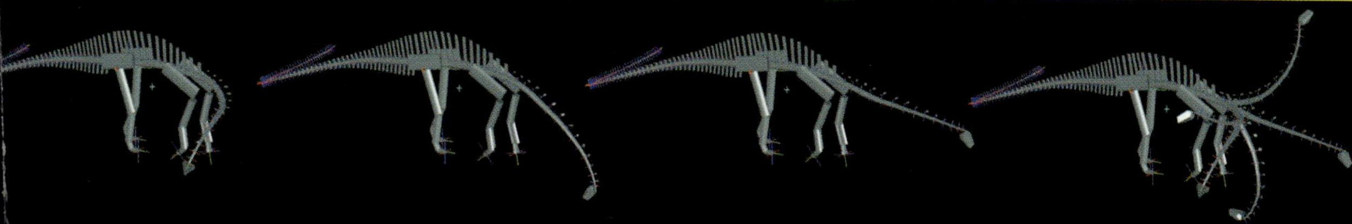

SAUCEPANS

Children enjoy collecting as a hobby, but what they collect changes over time. They often like to collect a full set of something by swapping with one another. Today, toy makers produce 'collectables' like sets of cards and stickers. During the Second World War, children's collections were very different.

These girls are collecting scrap metal for a Spitfire fighter plane. It took at least 2000 large saucepans to make a Spitfire!

COLLECTING IN WARTIME

During the Second World War, children collected comics, cigarette cards and marbles. Children also collected things that they found lying around, such as bottle tops.

During the war the government used trading cards to get across important wartime messages.

TO STICKERS

The government tried to focus children's collecting on things that would be useful to the war effort. They encouraged schools, youth groups and individual children to collect scrap metal. People were told that iron railings, pots and pans, tin cans - almost anything metal – would be melted down and turned into fighter airplanes. Not a children's collection!

A DANGEROUS HOBBY

Children also collected pieces of exploded bombs (shrapnel). This was very dangerous, because some bombs did not explode on hitting the ground. The unexploded bombs stayed hidden in the ground. Anything could set them off, especially a child scrambling around looking for shrapnel. Collecting things could be dangerous then!

Looking for shrapnel amongst the rubbish was great fun, but very dangerous.

What do people look for in a home? Somewhere safe and warm that's close to the shops? Well, animals are pretty much the same!

Different animals live in different habitats, such as mountains, meadows, forests or the sea. An animal's home needs to be safe from predators and to provide shelter in bad weather. It also needs to be near good supplies of food.

SQUIRREL

- Light nimble creature that lives in forests.
- Feeds on nuts and seeds.
- Sleeps a lot during the winter.

MOLE

- Small creature that lives under the ground.
- Strong front paws for burrowing through the soil.
- Feeds on worms and insects.

POLAR BEAR

- Strong and powerful animal.
- Lives in the Arctic.
- Females give birth to cubs during winter months.

BEAVER

- Water animal with strong jaws and sharp teeth.
- Lives in rivers and lakes.
- Hibernates during the winter.
- Hunted by bears and lynx.

WASP

- Flying insect with strong jaws.
- Lives in large family groups called colonies.
- Each colony raises thousands of young.

SEA ANEMONE

- Sea creature that looks like a plant.
- Anchors itself to underwater rocks.
- Uses its poisonous tentacles to catch fish.

Homes

Look at each of the animals on the left hand page and read about its life and habits. Can you match it with its correct home on the right hand page?

CORAL REEF
- A rocky structure made of tiny animals called corals.
- Found in warm, shallow, sunlit seas.
- Teems with fish and many other animals.

NEST
- Built of thin sheets of paper made from chewed-up wood.
- Found high off the ground.
- Contains thousands of tiny holes.

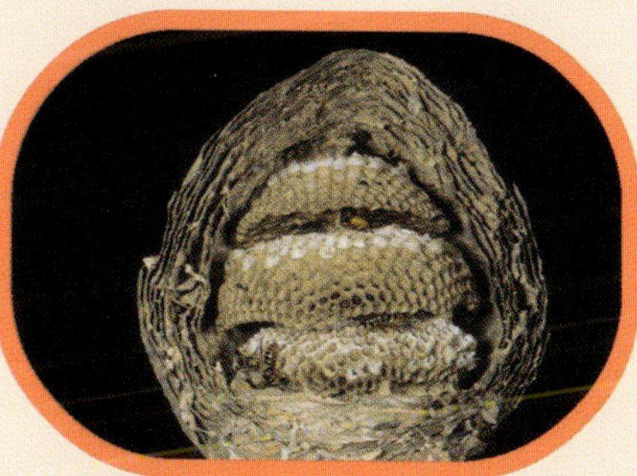

BURROW
- A network of tunnels under the soil.
- Gives protection from cold weather and predators.
- Close to worms and other creatures.

DAM
- A safe, dry shelter made of branches and mud.
- Found at the edge of lakes or in streams.
- Entered through underwater tunnels.

DREY
- A football-sized nest made of twigs, leaves and grass.
- Found in the forks of trees.
- Keeps out cold and wet weather.

SNOW DEN
- A large chamber dug into a deep snowdrift.
- Traps warm air and keeps out the cold.
- Gives protection from hungry predators.

Professor Gizmo's Money Boxes

Brilliant Professor Gizmo has been asked by the Hotshot Executive Toy Corporation to design a money box that will appeal to adults and children. The professor has come up with four designs, and today he has brought them to show Hotshot.

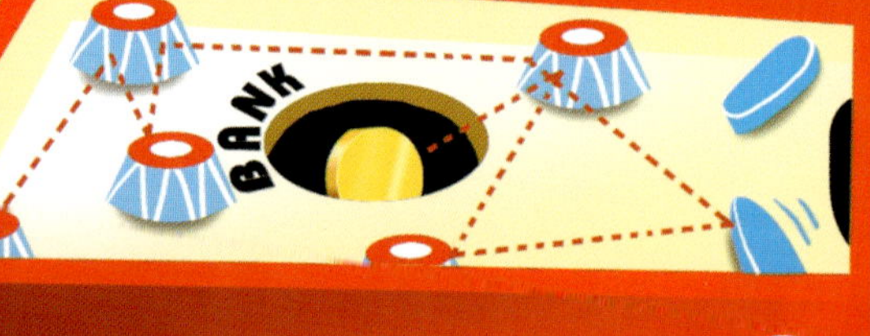

The Directors of the Hotshot Executive Toy Corporation can only choose one of the professor's clever money boxes if they are to manufacture it in time for Christmas. Which one do you think they'll go for?

Turn over the page to find out.

The Directors have decided to manufacture the Water Feature Money Box. They ask Professor Gizmo to show them exactly how it works.

The Directors also need to think about how they will advertise and sell the money box. Here are their ideas. Do you think it will be successful?

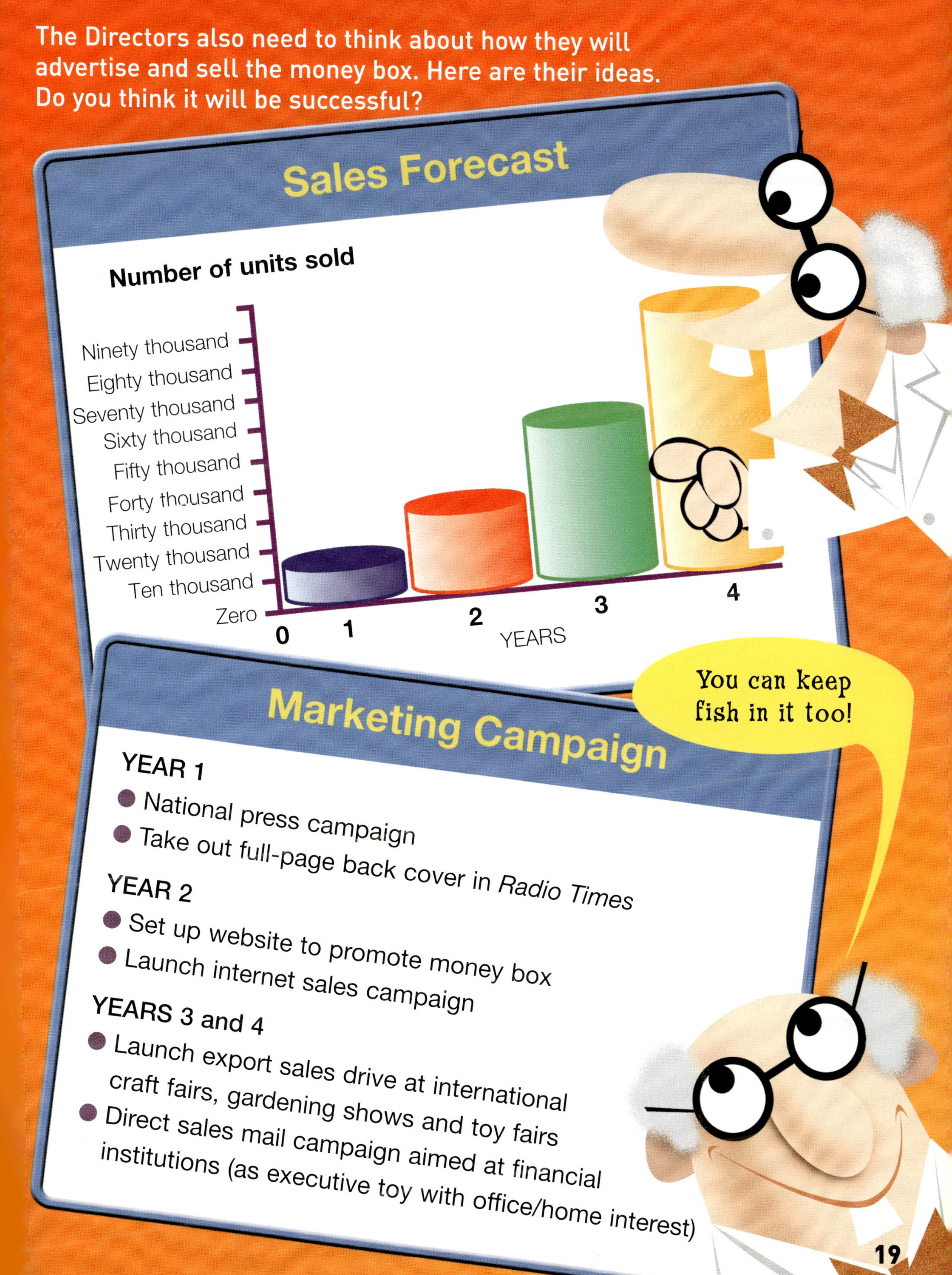

PUZZLING PICTURES

CAN I SEE THAT AGAIN?

Pictures sometimes play tricks on our eyes – we can see different things in them every time we look! Have a look at these pictures. What do you see?

IT WAS A BRIGHT MOONLIT NIGHT

This picture is called *New Year's Frolics*. It was painted in 1903 by a Norwegian artist called Theodor Kittelsen. What makes this picture more than a winter landscape in moonlight?

PICTURE THE PATTERN

This picture is called *Sky and Water*. It is a woodcut made by a Dutch artist called Maurits Cornelis Escher in 1938. What do you notice about the birds and the fish?

MAKING FACES

This picture is called *Autumn*. It was painted in the sixteenth century by an Italian artist called Giuseppi Arcimboldo.
Why do you think the picture is called *Autumn*? Can you work out what the artist has used to create his picture?

WHICH WAY?

Who do you see? Now look again – do you see someone else? How has the artist made two faces out of one picture?

UPSIDE DOWN?

What do you see when you look at this picture?
Now turn the picture upside down!

What do you see now?
How do you think the artist made two pictures out of one?

THE LIFE OF A HERO

Every day, all over the world, people go missing. Sometimes people just get lost. Sometimes they are trapped when a building collapses during an earthquake. Or they might be buried in snow after an avalanche.

What happens to these people? If they are lucky, they may be found by a search and rescue dog. These dogs are trained to follow the scent of a missing person.

Training search and rescue dogs takes a long time. Skylar, a German shepherd dog, started training when she was just three months old. Read on to find out how Madeline trained Skylar to be such a great search and rescue dog.

8 WEEKS OLD

Madeline tested three puppies to find out if they could be good search and rescue dogs. She took them to strange places. She played ball games with them. She made loud noises to see if this scared the dogs. Skylar passed all Madeline's tests.

3 MONTHS OLD

Skylar started her training. First, she went to puppy school to learn commands such as 'heel', 'sit down' and 'stay'. Madeline took Skylar everywhere with her, so that Skylar could get used to meeting new people.

8 MONTHS OLD

Next, Madeline and Skylar played hide-and-seek games. Madeline hid in different places, so that Skylar had to find her. Then Skylar learned to find strangers as well as people she knew.

18 MONTHS OLD

Finally, Skylar was ready to work as a search and rescue dog. But first she had to be tested. The judges checked that Skylar could follow the scent of different people. They watched Skylar and Madeline work together. Skylar passed the test with flying colours!

2 YEARS OLD

Skylar received her first call to action! Two boys were lost in the woods. Skylar ran through the woods, following the boys' scent. After about a mile, Skylar got very excited. She had found the boys! They had fallen asleep in the woods. This was the first of many successful rescues for Skylar and Madeline.

Is seeing believing?

Optical illusions are images that appear to show one thing – until you look more closely, that is! Then you find out that the picture shows something completely different.

What do you see in these pictures? Are you sure? Look again!

1 Which of the horizontal lines is longer, the top one or the bottom one?

2 Which step is the bottom and which is the top?

3 Which vertical line is longer?

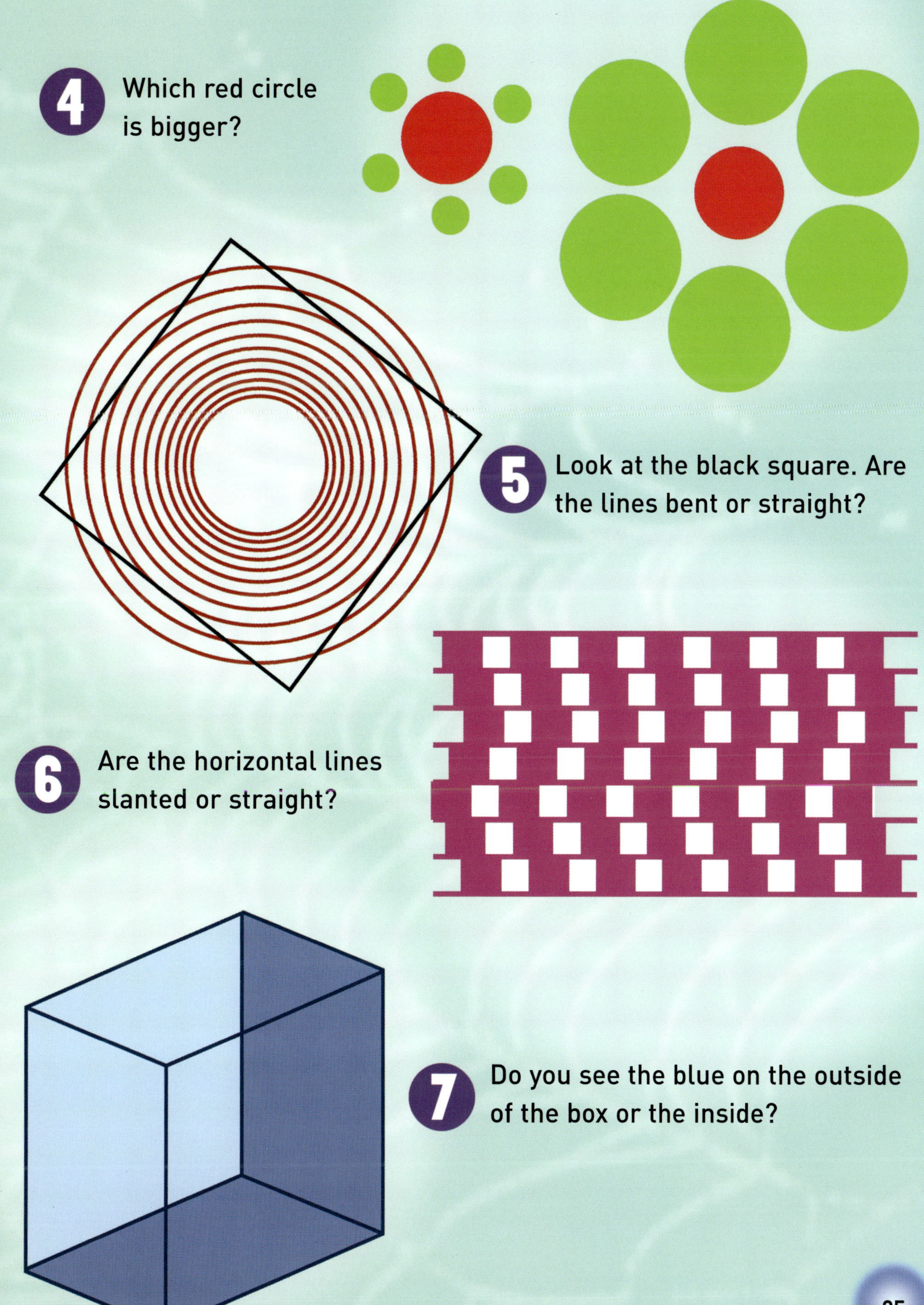

4 Which red circle is bigger?

5 Look at the black square. Are the lines bent or straight?

6 Are the horizontal lines slanted or straight?

7 Do you see the blue on the outside of the box or the inside?

Byte-Sized ICT

Aluminium – new cans from old

ICT: Unit 4a
Writing for different audiences

Can you recycle?

Could you encourage others to recycle their aluminium drinks cans? Have a go at designing a poster, using publishing software on your computer. Remember to include some information about why recycling is so important.

Your poster needs to be eye-catching. You should be able to read the main points from a distance away, so you will need to use large font sizes. You could also try using different colours to make the key points stand out more. Why not do a test print to try different colours and see which colours stand out the most?

Your computer will probably have some clip-art you can use to add pictures to your poster. You might even be able to find the recycling symbol.

Rutland under water

Setting out both sides

Read pages 8 and 9, then use a word-processor to type two lists:

1. A list of reasons why people were against Rutland Water being made.
2. A list giving reasons for the reservoir.

Try to keep your reasons short, by typing them in note form. You could use the 'bullet point' button to separate each reason. Why not type each list in a different colour to make it clear which is which? If you can think of any other reasons for and against that aren't mentioned, add them to your lists.

Finally, re-read your work and decide if you think Rutland Water was good idea or not. Type your view at the end, using a third colour.

Running with dinosaurs!

Dinosaur research challenge

Choose a dinosaur from the list on page 11. You could choose your favourite, or perhaps one you've never heard of before. Do some research using a CD-ROM or the Internet.

Can you find out six more facts about the dinosaur? Think about what it eats, how it moves and how it behaves. Can you find a picture of it to print out?

Animal homes

ICT: Unit 4c

Branching databases

Animal branches

How much have you learned about the animals on pages 14 and 15? Use a branching database program to sort them. Remember – you need to think of questions to divide them into two groups each time.

You could include the information about their homes as well as their habitat, and any features you can see on the photographs. It's always a good idea to check through the database at the end.

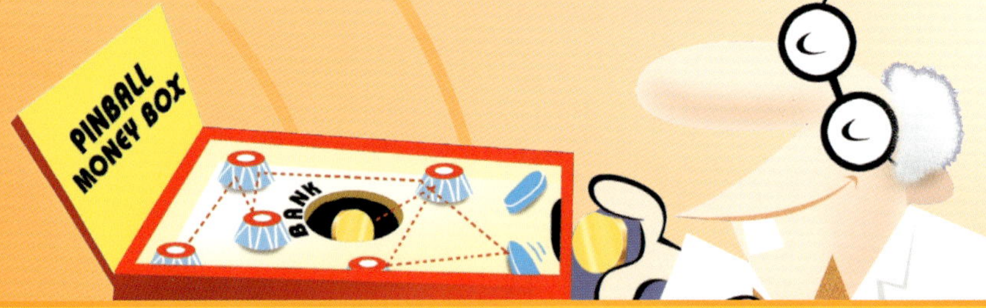

Professor Gizmo's money boxes

Design your own money box

Let your imagination run wild! Use the art program on your computer to design your own mega-cool money box. Think about including some unusual, wacky or downright ridiculous features!

Can you come up with an idea that is even more zany than Professor Gizmo's? Something that every child will want? Remember to include some labels to explain the fantastic features.

Puzzling pictures

Virtual art gallery

Do you want to see more pictures by famous artists without leaving your classroom? Check out the websites of a few galleries.

There are many pictures to see online, as well as information about artists. Most galleries allow you to search using an artist's name or the name of a picture, or you can simply browse the pictures online.

Alternatively, your school may have a CD-ROM of pictures by famous artists for you to view. Can you find out more about your favourite picture or artist?

Glossary

aluminium	a light thin silvery metal
archaeologist	someone who studies ancient remains, usually by excavation
Arctic	the north polar area
bauxite	the main mineral used to make aluminium
biped	a two-footed animal
colony	a group of the same type of animal living together
hibernate	some animals hibernate, or go to sleep, in the winter

osprey	a type of bird of prey
palaentologist	someone who studies life in the distant past (especially dinosaurs) through fossils
quadruped	a four-footed animal
recycling	the process of turning household waste into material that can be re-used
reservoir	an artificial lake made for water sports, or to store drinking water
vertebrae	the individual parts of the backbone

Index